Quick Travel Guide to

London

By Sarah Marie

The Contents

Introduction

London, the capital of the United Kingdom, is one of the world's financial, fashion, arts and entertainment capitals. The city's history can be traced back to Roman times. It includes the lives of such notable political figures as William the Conqueror, Thomas à Becket and Queen Elizabeth I. This haven has even included the most world-renowned authors like William Shakespeare, John Milton, Charles Dickens, Jane Austen and others who contributed to one of the world's greatest bodies of literature. London, once the capital of a great empire, was also a focal point of the Industrial Revolution around 1750, serving as a showcase for both material advancement and the social evils it spawned.

London is one of the most popular tourist destinations in the world, with a population of 8.6 million people. According to the NPI, just 40% of London's population is British, while the other 60% is made up of people of various nationalities, making the city extremely diverse. People from many walks of life can be found speaking a variety of languages across the city.

All of this diversity brings together a wide range of civilizations in one location. Walking down a random city block, you'll find an English pub, a burger joint along with an array of Italian, Indian, Thai and Chinese restaurants, as well as a variety of other cuisines.

Because England is an English-speaking country, there is generally no language barrier. Even though English is English, there are some slang phrases which are not used in the United States. It's critical not to become perplexed. When they mention chips, they don't necessarily mean potato chips. When it comes to chips, you must try fish and chips at least once, if not ten times.

In terms of transportation, navigating the tube, buses and trains (aided by several excellent apps) is a breeze. Become accustomed to the phrase "Mind the Gap," which is an audible or visual warning phrase issued to rail passengers to take caution while crossing the horizontal, and in some cases vertical, spatial gap between the train door and the station platform.

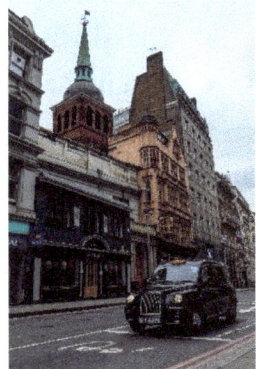

This ain't no Uber in London. When there, it is a treat to take London's black cabs. As Uber and Lyft takes over the city, these great cabbies are a dying breed and should be cherished. The amazement of London black cabs, is the people driving go to school for two years to train as well as knowing every city street and the knowledge of all of London.

With no worries about transportation, it's simple to travel around and visit all London's magnificent historical (and non-historical) sights. The city is bursting with intriguing attractions to see and learn about, whether it's the Tower of London or the London Eye. There are over 100 museums, galleries and exhibits to visit. All of which provide insight into London's fascinating history.

Here's a list of things to do in London if you ever get the chance:

- Photo of a red phone booth
- Big Ben for a selfie
- Classic fish and chips supper
- Tea in the afternoon at a café
- Ride through Hyde Park
- Say "Cheers!" as thank you as many times as possible (you'll immediately seem like a local)
- Watch the Changing of the Guard
- Buckingham Palace
- British Museum
- Westminster Abbey
- Pictures of Old and New Architecture

Amazing History of London, England

London is the capital city of the United Kingdom. It is both one of the world's oldest and most cosmopolitan cities, with a history spanning nearly two millennia. It is not just the country's largest metropolis, but also its economic, transportation and cultural hub.

London is located in Southeastern England, 50 miles upstream from the Thames estuary on the North Sea. The metropolis may be seen compactly within a green belt of open land in satellite pictures, with its main ring route (the M25 motorway) threading around it at a radius of around 20 miles from the city center.

In the mid-1950s, rigorous town planning limitations slowed the growth of the built-up region. Its physical boundaries roughly correlate to the administrative and statistical boundaries separating Greater London from the "home counties" of Kent, Surrey and Berkshire to the south of the river. Buckinghamshire, Hertfordshire and Essex to the north of the river. The historic counties of Kent, Hertfordshire and Essex cover a large portion of the metropolitan county of Greater London, which was established in 1965.

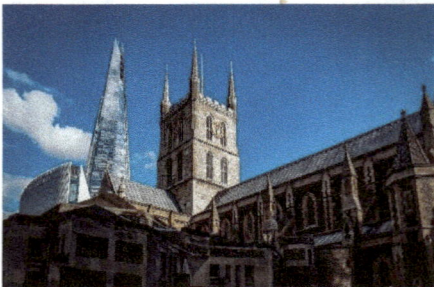

The walled settlement founded by the Romans on the banks of the Thames in the first century CE, now known as the City of London, "the Square Mile," or simply "the City." The suburb of Southwark faces across the bridge on the lower gravels of the south bank. The City of Westminster is a mile upstream on a great southward bend of the river. The three villages have a unique and complementary purpose. London grew as a center of trade, commerce and banking. Southwark, or "the Borough," became famed for its monasteries, hospitals, inns, fairs, pleasure houses and Elizabethan London's great theatres—the Rose (1587), the Swan (1595) and the world-famous Globe (1599).

Westminster sprang established around an abbey, which brought with it a royal palace and, in turn, the full British state apparatus—legislature, administration and judiciary. It also has large parks. The West End has one of the most desirable areas for living and shopping. In the early 17th century, the north-bank communities united into a single built-up region, although they did not join into a single expanded municipality. The City of London was the only capital city in Europe to retain its medieval limits. As London grew in size and became the template of the contemporary metropolis, Westminster and other suburbs were left to build their own administrative structures—a process that was repeated a hundred times over.

Fun Facts

The City of London is Ancient – And Tiny

The ancient centre of the British capital is only 1.12 square miles in size. Locals refer to it as the Square Mile. This was London when the Romans arrived in the first century AD and stayed until the Middle Ages.

The City of London is now a tiny, teeny-little section of the metropolis, and it is England's smallest county.

In London, almost 300 Languages are Spoken

This is one of those bizarre London facts! London is home to a varied spectrum of people and cultures as a result of its long history of immigration. The dialect of London is diverse, ranging from Kurdish to Korean.

London is the Center of the World

Well, sort of. Specifically, Greenwich. This historic area is where you'll find the Royal Observatory. This defines 0° longitude (i.e., the Prime Meridian) and Greenwich Mean Time (GMT).

That's what you probably know as Coordinated Universal Time or UTC, but GMT predates this term by over 300 years.

The London Underground is the World's Oldest Underground Railway System

It may be rough-around-the-edges, lack air-con and cell phone signals, but the London Underground is a pioneer of traveling by train under the ground.

In January 1863, a line between Paddington and Farringdon was opened. The carriages were wooden, gas-lit and pulled by steam locomotives.

London Wasn't a Healthy Place in the 17th Century

There were many diseases circulating in London at the time - diseases far worse than the

flu. The Great Plague, a horrible epidemic of the bubonic plague, killed roughly 100,000 individuals between 1665 and 1666. It was over a quarter of London's population at the time.

The Great Fire of London Started in a Bakery

... not to mention on Pudding Lane. It happened in the year 1666. The fire started shortly after midnight on Sunday, September 2, and soon spread over London, destroying roughly a fifth of the city.

This included the Cathedral of St. Paul. The obvious result was a brick-and-stone makeover for the city.

London was the World's Largest City From 1831 to 1925

That's correct. This fascinating London fact claims that it was the world's greatest metropolis for nearly a century, exceeding

Beijing's population of 1.1 million in the mid-1800s and reaching a population of 7,419,000 by 1914. New York City took over after that. London is now the world's 33rd most populous city.

Number 10 Downing Street is Over 300 Years Old

This is the British White House. It has about 100 rooms and a private apartment on the third floor, as well as a kitchen in the basement.

Foreign dignitaries can be met at offices on higher levels. Larry, a mouse-catching cat, is also a resident.

"One of the World's Greenest Cities" is London.

This is one of the most interesting London facts! At least, according to the London Natural History Society. It has over 40% of open space, 2,000 species of blooming plants, 120 species of fish in the Thames, 60 species of birds breeding in Central London, 47 species of butterfly, 270 types of spiders and 1,173 moths. London can be classified as a forest under EU standards!

London Slang

- Guv'nor (or simply "Guv") – This is a contraction of the word "Governor," and equates to American words including "chief," "mac" or "buddy." It's a friendly term used to refer to anyone from a stranger to a life-long acquaintance
- All right? – A greeting that means "hello, how are you?"
- Cheers – Used frequently instead of "thank you" or "goodbye." It's also spoken to celebrate a toast.
- Ta – "Thank you" not to be confused with "Ta-Ta," which means goodbye.
- Khazii – Toilet / restroom
- Bloke - "Bloke" would be the American English equivalent of "dude." It means a "man."
- Lad - In the same vein as "bloke," "lad" is used, however, for boys and younger men.
- Bonkers - Not necessarily intended in a bad way, "bonkers" means "mad" or "crazy."
- Daft - Used to mean if something is a bit stupid. It's not particularly offensive, just a mildly silly or foolish piece of UK slang.
- To leg it - This term means to run away, usually from some trouble! "I legged it from the police."
- Trollied / Plastered - These two words are British slang for drunk. One can get creative here and just add "ed" to the end of practically any object to get across the same meaning eg. hammered.

12

- Quid - This is British slang for British pounds. Some people also refer to it as "squid."
- Dodgy - This England slang word is used to describe something or someone a little suspicious or questionable. For example, it can refer to food which tastes out of date or, when referring to a person, it can mean that they are a bit sketchy.
- Gobsmacked - This is a truly British expression. "Gobsmacked" means to be utterly shocked or surprised beyond belief. "Gob" is a British expression for "mouth."

- Bevvy - This is short for the word "beverages," usually alcoholic, most often beer.

- Knackered - "Knackered" is used when someone is extremely tired. For example, "I was up studying all night last night, I'm absolutely knackered."

- Lost the plot - Someone who has "lost the plot" has become either angry, irrational, or is acting ridiculously. For example, "When my dad saw the mess I made, he lost the plot."

- Taking the piss - This is one of the most commonly used British slang phrases. To "take the piss" means to mock, or generally be sarcastic towards something. For example, "Don't be so serious, I was only taking the piss." Not to be confused with "being pissed."

- Pissed - The British sure do love their bevvys. This is one of the many British terms for being drunk

- Throwing a wobbly - This British expression means to have a tantrum, however, tends to be used when describing tantrums thrown by adults, or people who should otherwise know better.

- A cuppa - A cuppa is the shortened version of "a cup of tea." You might hear the expression "fancy a cuppa?" quite often which is normally always referring to tea. The British do love their tea after all!

- Bloody - As British slang, "bloody" places emphasis on a comment or another word. "That's bloody brilliant!" for example. It is regarded as a mild expletive (swear word) but due to its common usage, it is generally acceptable. For example, "Oh bloody hell!"

- Can't be arsed - A commonly used British slang sentence is "Can't be arsed." This is a less polite version of saying that you can't be bothered doing something. You might also see this abbreviated to "CBA" in textspeak.

- Chuffed - If someone is "chuffed," they are very happy or delighted.

- Skint - "Skint" is a British expression to mean being broke or having no money. Lacking "fivers" and "tenners" if you will.

- Fiver - A five-pound note.

- Tenner - A ten-pound note.

- Bog - Not a muddy marsh, but a toilet. Oh, the British!

- Bog roll - These British words refer to the paper you use in the bog, also known as "toilet paper."

- Bird - This is British slang for a girl or a woman.

- Mug - "Mug" is more specifically London slang and is associated with the cockney accent. This is not a particularly nice word to describe someone as it means a fool or a stupid person.

- Chav - This is a derogatory British slang word for a young hooligan who normally starts fights and makes trouble. "Chavs" are usually seen as lower class.

- Git - "Git" is a British expression of insult. It's chav slang to describe a person, usually a man, who is very unpleasant, incompetent, or is an idiot.

- Cheeky - This is used to describe someone's behavior. If someone is being "cheeky," they are being slightly rude or disrespectful but in a charming or amusing way. If you are a "cheeky" child, you are being brash or disrespectful and will probably get into trouble.

- Slag off - To "slag someone off" means to make fun of a person by verbally attacking them.

- Sod - This British expression shares a similar meaning to "devil" or "thing" and is used to refer to a person, particularly a man. "You stupid sod!" or "You lucky sod!"

- Grafting - "Grafting" is Scottish slang denoting a lad who is trying to get a girl to like him. A bit like flirting. You'll hear this one a lot on the British Love Island.

- Muppet - Another great British insult. A "muppet" is a person who is ignorant and is generally a bit clueless.

- Pants - In the UK, "pants" typically refers to underwear. However, "pants" can also be used as an equivalent of the word "bad" e.g. "That's pants!"

- Prat - Yet another classic British slang term of insult. A "prat" is someone who is full of themselves and, almost invariably, stupid as well. With a hint of delusion.

- Nosh - "That's real good nosh!" "Nosh" is a British expression for "food."

- Buzzin' - "Buzzin'" can mean to be tipsy or slightly drunk, "I'm buzzin' after that pint." It's also British slang for being excited or very happy, "I just booked my holiday to Spain, I'm absolutely buzzin'."

- Pied off - This is not a nice feeling. If you've been "pied off," you've been rejected or shot down.

- Bev - This one had most of us confused when we first heard it on Love Island 2019. "Bev" means a "handsome man."

- To crack on - "To crack on with something" means to get started or continue with something. To use these UK slang words in a sentence you'd say, "It's getting late, I better crack on."

- Gutted - Meaning of being bitterly disappointed about something. "I was absolutely gutted when I heard the bad news."

- Blimey - "Blimey" is used as a way of expressing surprise at something, "Blimey, look at that!"

- Cock-up - Get your mind out of the gutter! A "cock-up" is a mistake or failure, "I made a total cock-up of it."

- Kerfuffle - If you've gotten yourself into a "kerfuffle," you are generally involved in a disagreement with someone. "Kerfuffle" also has a similar meaning to "fuss." For example, you can say, "It was all a big kerfuffle."

- Innit - This is one of the most commonly heard UK slangs. It's the shortened and easier version of "isn't it?" It's seen as a general filler in a conversation or when seeking confirmation, eg. "Cool, innit."

- Cracking - When something or someone is "cracking" it means that the thing or the person is particularly good or excellent. For example, "He's a cracking lad" or "That's a cracking cuppa."

- Minging - This is British slang for "disgusting" or "gross."

- Proper - "Proper" is used as an alternative to "very" or "extremely." For example, "That's proper good nosh, innit."

- To nick - This is a British expression to mean stealing. As in "I nicked these sweets from the shop."

- Faffing around - "Faffing around" is a very British pleasure. It means doing nothing particularly productive or taking unnecessary time to do something that should be relatively quick or straightforward.

British Etiquette Tips

At the best of times, knowing how to act responsibly in social situations can be tough. It's much more difficult when visiting a foreign country such as the United Kingdom, which is known for its rigid British etiquette rules.

While books and media can teach you a lot, nothing beats mingling with locals and seeing their habits for understanding a country. Here are a few basic suggestions for navigating the minefield of British etiquette to get you started.

Complaining

The British love to whine! They'll gleefully complain about the lousy weather and pricey cuisine to one another. When people have a genuine problem with a product or experience poor treatment, they are less adept at complaining. When they do, they do so with a sense of regret. Even when they are complaining, British people remain courteous!

Queuing

Across the UK, Brits are frequently observed forming orderly queues. They'll be at the front of the line at the grocery, the railway station, or a performance. Queue-jumping or moving ahead in line, is the biggest error anybody can make. Those who have been patiently waiting for this will always be disappointed.

Being Polite

In British etiquette, saying "please" and "thank you" are two crucial things to remember. Politeness and good manners are always appreciated, regardless of who you're interacting with.

Table Manners

Table manners differ from country to country. Each country has its own views about how to act during a meal, from slurping to burping. Although formal settings have their own set of regulations, remember to eat slowly, set your silverware down between bites and never speak with your mouth full.

Tipping

Even Brits have trouble deciding how much to tip a server at cafés and restaurants, or whether they should tip at all. After your meal, always check your bill. If it says "service not included," it indicates you can leave a gratuity for the person who served you. The amount is entirely up to you. It is usual to add an extra 10% to the bill total if the service was excellent. Many British people tip taxi drivers and hairdressers, however, the exact amount is up to the consumer.

Using Mobile Phones in Public

Even though mobile phones are a part of everyday life, there are still unwritten rules to follow when using them. Using a cellphone at the dining table, as well as speaking loudly while on the phone, is considered disrespectful, especially on public transportation.

Good Sportsmanship

Nobody likes a loser, as the saying goes. Sulking, disputing or whining after losing in any type of competition is considered impolite. Whether you've been outclassed on the sports field or in the classroom, no matter how unhappy you are, thank your opponent graciously.

Drunkenness

Drinking alcohol can be laden with dos and don'ts depending on the situation. Moderation is always recommended. If you've had one too many drinks, try to avoid becoming aggressive, emotional or disrespectful.

Chivalry

Traditional chivalry and etiquette rules still apply. For example, in Britain, holding a door open for a lady and standing up when entering a room for the first time are still considered polite.

Apologizing

The British's love of apologizing, no etiquette book would be complete. Although, one might expect to apologize for stomping on a shopper's toe or colliding with a passer-by, many people will be astonished to learn when two Brits get into a fight, each will apologize for getting in the way of the other. They are unconcerned about who is to blame. Many of life's minor mishaps are met with an automatic apology. This is a British characteristic!

Top Attractions

Visit the Crown Jewels at the Tower of London

The Tower of London, which dates back to the 1070s, has served as a fortification, prison, royal mint and even a zoo over the years. It is now a major tourist destination and the home of the crown jewels. It is also the only castle in inner London, allowing you to cross another item off your bucket list: seeing an English castle.

Watch Tower Bridge Lift Up for Passing Ships

Tower Bridge is frequently misidentified as London Bridge (which is the next bridge to the west and significantly less stunning!). Most people are unaware it raises on a regular basis to allow ships to pass! Make sure to check the Tower Bridge website for lift timings and schedule your visit to see the bridge open!

View the Houses of Parliament and the Westminster Palace.

The Houses of Parliament is possibly the most well-known of all London attractions. It is the British government's gathering location and is officially known as the Palace of Westminster.

Set Your Clock to Big Ben's Chime

The Elizabeth Tower is the name of the tower you will be staring at. The moniker 'Big Ben' was given to the Great Bell at first, but it has since come to be associated with the bell, the tower, and the clock.

Wave to the King at Buckingham Palace

Buckingham Palace is the King's official residence. Admire the palace's opulence, and if you're lucky, you might even catch a peek of His Majesty!

Tours of certain of the palace's staterooms are available at specific periods of the year. For further information, see the Buckingham Palace website or combine a palace visit with a walking tour.

Witness the Changing of the Guard

Witnessing the changing of the guard is an incredibly popular thing to do for foreigners visiting London.

It only takes place on certain days, so check on the Changing Guard website for up-to-date info regarding times and the best places to watch the ceremony. If you prefer, you can book a tour that will show you the best locations to view the parade, as well as provide more information about its history.

Feel like Royalty Along the Mall

The Mall is one of London's most well-known streets. It's the road that leads up to Buckingham Palace. It's painted red to look like a long red carpet!

Visit Westminster Abbey

Dating back to 960, Westminster Abbey is a true London icon and cannot be missed. It has been the official place of coronation since 1066. As one of four UNESCO sites in London, Westminster Abbey is a must-see in London.

Admire the views from Westminster Bridge

The London Eye and South Bank are visible on one side of the Thames, while the Houses of Parliament and Big Ben are visible on the other architecture.

Snap a Photo of the London Eye

Riding the London Eye is on a lot of people's London bucket lists but a lot of tourists think it's a waste of money. Unless you have a combined ticket with other attractions including entry at no additional cost.

It is easily one of the most Instagrammable places in London so soak in the views of it from various angles and get that perfect insta-worthy shot!

Explore London's South Bank

A riverside stroll down the South Bank will not only provide you with stunning views across the River Thames of many of London's landmarks, but it will also introduce you to a plethora of restaurants, bars, ancient pubs, market stalls and street entertainers.

Marvel at St Paul's Cathedral

St. Paul's Cathedral is an architectural marvel that was once London's tallest structure. None of the other great churches in London can compare to St. Paul!

Many sights surrounding the city block views of St. Paul's. At the very least, go around the outside of the magnificent church to see its intricate details and majesty.

If you have the time, you should go inside as well. When you purchase tickets in advance, you save money and get to skip the wait.

Walk Across Millennium Bridge

Millennium Bridge was built in the year 2000, as its name suggests. This magnificent steel suspension footbridge was the first to cross the River Thames in almost a century.

If you look closely as you cross the bridge, you could just spot one of London's hidden beauties! Ben Wilson's tiny, concealed pieces of art painted on chewing gum can be found all over the bridge.

Climb the Great Fire of London Monument.

The Monument to the Great Fire of London was planned by Christophe Wren and completed in 1677 to commemorate the Great Fire of London and to celebrate the city's reconstruction. You can climb the 311 steps to the summit for stunning views of the city if you're physically capable.

Enjoy a Moment of Peace at St. Dunstan in the East

St. Dunstan in the East is a little oasis nestled in the heart of London. Just a short walk from the Tower of London and you can escape the hustle and bustle of the city within the beautiful church remains and garden.

Visit the Lions at Trafalgar Square

…And visit the smallest police station in Britain!

Trafalgar Square is home to four massive brass lion sculptures as well as the world's tiniest police station. The lions are more difficult to climb aboard than they appear.

Watch the Street Performers in Covent Garden

Covent Garden offers a variety of activities, including fantastic shops, restaurants and bars. The street entertainers, on the other hand, are what make this section of London so enjoyable. A number of them can be found in and around the main square and neighboring streets.

There are also numerous charming lanes with bespoke boutique businesses to explore. Many of them make you feel as though you've walked away from the capital and into a small English village!

Surround Yourself in Color at Neals Yard

This vibrant little courtyard is surrounded with stores and restaurants and is normally considerably quieter than the surrounding regions, providing a welcome break from the city's turmoil! It also makes for a great Instagram image in London.

Explore Chinatown

Chinatown is a hotspot of Chinese culture in the heart of London, centered around Gerrard Street. There are many Chinese restaurants and small shops, as well as streets painted with Chinese motifs such as dragons and lanterns. Make a point of visiting the Chinese gate on Wardour Street, which was constructed in Beijing and placed in 2016.

Enjoy Cocktails and Nightlife in Soho

Popular with Londoners and tourists alike, Soho is the perfect place to enjoy London nightlife. It's a diverse, vibrant area with many great restaurants, bars and clubs. Parts of Soho also have a very risqué vibe with not-so-subtle sex shops and burlesque.

Take in the Lights Piccadilly Circus

Piccadilly Circus (on a smaller scale!) is London's answer to Times Square. It's a terrific area to roam about at night and just take in the buzz.

People Watch in Leicester Square

Leicester Square is another tourist favorite, and because of this it can be a bit of a tourist trap. Definitely avoid eating at the restaurants around here as they're typically overpriced. However, it's a great place to people watch or enjoy a cocktail with a view at the bar at Hotel Indigo.

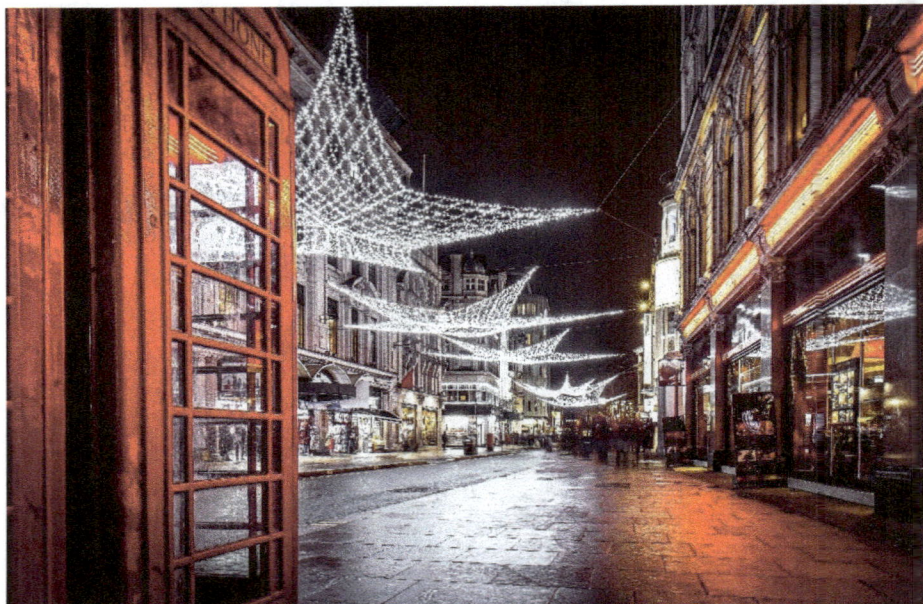

Fly Over the Thames on the Emirates Cable Car

The Emirates Airline Cable Car provides a unique perspective of London, with views of the O2 Arena and the metropolitan skyline. By definition, this information is ephemeral; if you can, check out one of the many dedicated blogs for the most up-to-date information.

Unleash Your Inner child at Ballie Ballerson

Ballie Ballerson has London's first (and only) adult ball pit. At this playful pub, immerse yourself in a sea of color while sipping a cocktail and letting your inner child loose.Rive

Take a Cruise Along the River Thames

London is a beautiful city from any angle, but it's particularly impressive from the water. Take a sight-seeing cruise along the Thames or hop on the Thames Clipper to take in some of the best sights from the river.

Hidden Gems

London is much more than the Thames River and a few tourist photos. Though the Houses of Parliament and huge museums such as the Natural History Museum are must-sees on every trip to London. There are plenty of eccentric London sites to see as well. The city is full of hidden jewels just waiting to be discovered...

This is your complete guide to strange, distinctive, quirky and offbeat things in London, from what to eat to where to go.

Temple District, London EC4Y 7BB

This set of passageways, secret alleyways and churches are located in the very heart of the capital, just minutes away from the embankment of the Thames River. The history of the secluded courtyard, Temple Church and the other ancient buildings date back hundreds of years and even has links to the Knights Templar.

This order is even said to have built Temple Church themselves. You can't go wrong by dedicating an hour or two to wandering the pedestrian-only streets, visiting the Church and snapping pictures of the secret gardens that make up this tiny little spot in central London. Nearby, this free and self-guided walking tour of London will help you explore another side of the city.

Leadenhall Market, Gracechurch St, London EC3V 1LT

The stunning Victorian architecture of Leadenhall Market is worth a visit, even if simply to see the amazing architecture and gorgeous tones of the buildings. It is best visited earlier in the day to avoid the crowds. The covered market, which was built on the location of the original Roman heart of 'Londinium,' is now home to a variety of vintage boutiques and independent stores and was even featured in Harry Potter.

The history of selling and market booths date all the way back to the 14th century, making it one of the city's oldest markets. The Temple of Mithras, a hidden jewel of the City of London next to Leadenhall Market, offers much more history. Long neglected, the Roman ruins have been reopened to the public thanks to a recent repair initiative.

Sir John Soane Museum, 13 Lincoln's Inn Fields, London WC2A 3BP

The Sir John Soane's Museum is located in Lincoln's Inn Fields and is small and quirky. Sir John Soane, a 19th-century architect and collector, once referred to this house museum as his "home." He left the house to the country when he died.

This museum is odd, unusual, and offbeat in every way. It is well worth a visit if you enjoy art, history, or anything Classical.

The collections are kept in a 19th-century structure designed to show off all of the arts and ornaments to their full potential. Soane gave the mansion and the items stored within it to the nation through an act of Parliament after his death in 1837.

One of the best things about the museum is it has a strict no-phone and no-photography policy, which means you can focus on the exhibits without being distracted.

The Smallest Police Station in the UK, Trafalgar Square, London WC2N 5DN

The smallest police station in England is hidden in plain sight in one of the busiest squares of London. Located on the corner of Trafalgar Square, the police box dates all the way back to the 1920s. Chiseled out of a repurposed lamp post, it provides secretive views over the entire square. Though it may not be officially recognized, it's still worth a peek if you're ever passing the area…

St. Bartholomew's the Great, Cloth Fair, London EC1A 7JQ

Of all the secret spots in London on this list, the church of St Bartholomew's the Great is a favorite. Situated in a little-known area, despite being so central, St Bartholomew's the Great is one of the oldest churches in the city and is home to stained glass windows, beautiful carvings and even its own set of cloisters.

Dating all the way back to Norman times, the church you see today was founded in 1123. Wander the cloisters and see architecture dating back hundreds of years. Nearby, you'll find hidden London gems such as the Golden Boy of Pye Corner and the Charterhouse.

'Roman' Bath House off the Strand, 5 Strand Ln, London WC2R 1AP

The Bath House, located off the Strand, is an unique piece of history that is most likely a "fake Roman bath house." The bath is worth a look even if it isn't much to look at (the title 'bath' is a little fancy for what is essentially a cement basin), if only to learn more about its fascinating history.

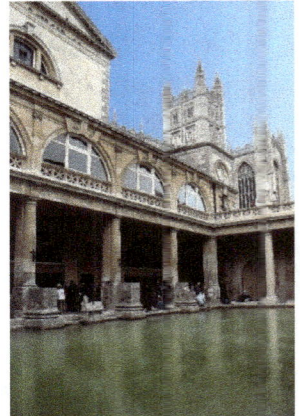

Strand & Aldwych Station, 171 Strand, London WC2R 1EP

Some London secret sites are so cleverly hidden that they are rarely visited. They're so overlooked that hundreds, if not thousands, of people walk past them every day without even recognizing they're there. The abandoned tube station of Strand and Aldwych is one of these places.

It's only one of many examples. After all, the city is littered with abandoned and decommissioned tube stations. While many are almost completely boarded up, several are still in use as film props or even as guided tours. Aldwych tube station has appeared in television and film productions including as *Sherlock*, *28 Weeks Later*, and *Mr. Selfridge*.

Dr. Johnson's House, 17 Gough Square, London EC4A 3DE

Though visiting a museum isn't the most uncommon thing to do in London, this museum is off the main path and pretty interesting.

The Grade I building can be found deep down a quiet tiny alleyway behind Temple's district. In reality, Johnson wrote the dictionary in one of its earlier forms in one of the rooms in the center of number 17, Gough Square.

The Tulip Stairs, Queen's House, Romney Rd, Greenwich, London SE10 9NF

If you're wanting to escape the hustle and bustle of the city for a day, then you might consider heading East of the city and towards Greenwich. This beautiful district of London is home to unusual London attractions such as the Greenwich Observatory, the Cutty Sark Ship and even the Prime Meridian Time Line (the exact point zero from which all times on Earth are measured).

For those who are searching for cultural attractions, the National Maritime Museum is the largest museum of its kind, while the Queen's House is all remains of a once Royal Residence. Today, it's free to visit many of these museums

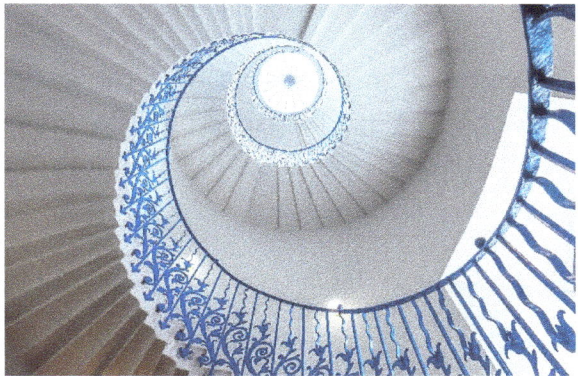

and a wander inside the Queen's House will guarantee the chance to spot the Tulip Stairs, the oldest set of self-supporting spiral stairs in Britain.

The Secrets of Hampton Court Palace

Though King Henry VIII's Palace is unquestionably one of London's most popular day tours, the former Royal Residence has a long and illustrious history. As a result, when it comes to this small piece of history, hidden gems and secret sites are never far away.

Did you know that the world's largest and oldest vine may be found in a greenhouse on the grounds of the palace? Or that another great king who lived in Hampton Court was the relatively forgotten Queen Anne? Anne constructed an entire Baroque wing to the chapel during her reign! The story of the Midnight Flit ought to be told somewhere else in the Palace...

Gordon's Wine Bar

Gordon's is the only wine bar in town for a drink with friends or a romantic date night. Easily one of London's best-kept secrets, this gem of a bar is set against the backdrop of historic wine barrel cellars and sells only one thing: wine.

While the cozy tables inside are made from ancient wine barrels, there is also plenty of sitting outside for those hot summer nights. If you get hungry, there are cheese and cold cut boards available. Otherwise, attend earlier in the evening rather than later, as the limited space fills up quickly!

Word on the Water, London's only 'book barge'

Word on the Water, which floats on a canal near King's Cross, is definitely one of London's oddest and most beautiful booksellers. The permanent location of this

boat at Granary Square, which is open seven days a week, is a relatively new phenomenon. Due to licensing issues in the past, the boat had to travel around on a very regular basis!

Museums

British Museum

You could spend several lifetimes in the British Museum, Britain's largest museum, without running out of artifacts to ponder. The collection is one of the largest in the world, arranged by location, and the list of big

hitters includes the Rosetta Stone and other finds from Ancient Egypt, Asia and the Middle East. Come early on a weekday for a less crowded experience, pick one gallery and stick to it (or go for a guided "Highlights" tour), and plan to hit one of the day's free 30-minute taster talks.

National Gallery

Set in London's busiest open space, Trafalgar Square, this is the grandmother of galleries with more than 2,300 paintings spanning the 13th to the 19th centuries: Heavyweights include Van

Gogh's *Sunflowers,* Velazquez's *Rokeby Venus,* and Constable's six-foot long *The Hay Wain*. It gets packed at weekends, but it's so large you can usually find a quiet corner. You can download an audio tour covering the museum's highlights, but you can also curate your own by selecting the paintings you want to see before you arrive.

Victoria and Albert Museum

South Kensington's V&A is one of the world's largest art and design museums, and arguably London's most glamorous. (Just the building itself is well worth the visit: a glorious red-brick palace filled with sculptural details, extravagant tiling, and frescos.) The collection is helpfully broken down into topics—fashion, theatre, furniture, architecture—and all are comprehensive, usually spanning several hundred (if not thousand) years.

Tate Modern

This former oil-fired power station sits smugly in the center of the South Bank, knowing that you're interested in what's going on inside. It's filled to the rafters with paintings and sculptures by the likes of Picasso, Dali, Warhol, and Rothko, all set off perfectly by gritty industrial interior.

Charles Dickens Museum

Charles Dickens' novels come to life inside this elegant Georgian townhouse where the author lived for a handful of years. More than 100,000 objects—including original manuscripts, letters and portraits—give an insight into the life of one of Britain's most famous writers, while the blue dining room, with its elaborate gold curtains, is a highlight; the table is set as if waiting for the Dickens family to come down for tea.

Churchill War Rooms

This underground lair, just around the corner from 10 Downing Street, is where Churchill spent endless hours plotting Allied victory during the Second World War. Come for the Map Room, which looks exactly as it did when the members of the War Cabinet abandoned it at the end of the war. The Transatlantic Telephone Room was where Churchill had secret conversations with U.S. officials. The audio guide comes with your ticket and provides an extra insight into the operations that went on during the war, including sounds and speeches of the time.

Design Museum

Inside the Design Museum, it's all minimalist, contemplative oak, and marble from which colorful, chaotic exhibitions explode. The permanent collection, "Designer, Maker, User," is a brilliant introduction to contemporary design including 1,000 objects, illustrating 20th and 21st-century architectural engineering and digital progress.

Horniman Museum and Gardens

The Horniman's far-out location (almost an hour from central London) means you can expect lots of lovely breathing space at a museum that would otherwise be packed. The huge building, with its looming clocktower, looks a bit like a very ornate train station and is surrounded by 16 acres of garden. You'll find large natural history and anthropology galleries, as well as an aquarium, carefully curated wild-looking gardens, and a beautiful Victorian conservatory.

Best Restaurants

Spring

Spring, located in the great neo-classical Somerset House, features a lovely dining area with pastel colors, Italian marble and flowering wall art is light-filled during the day and softly glowing at night. A rotating menu of a dozen starters and main courses highlight the finest of what's in season, which is frequently cultivated on Fern Verrow's 16-acre biodynamic farm. Skye Gyngell's meals are often Italian-inspired, but she's a culinary magpie, so labneh, persimmon and pickled chilis all make appearances. It's a delectably grown-up place to eat dinner: pricey, quietly elegant and unconcerned with trends.

Black Axe Mangal

Black Axe is a small, dimly lighted joint with a heavy metal addiction. With black and gold walls, waving lucky cats, and floral plastic tablecloths, the ambiance is "dive bar meets Chinese takeaway," yet there's considerable expertise in the (small) kitchen in the form of Lee Tiernan. Come for a dinner packed with flavors, spices and offal, with every component slow-cooked, created, or smoked in-house or a kid-friendly breakfast of cinnamon-banana flatbreads. Fast, friendly and appropriately rock 'n' roll service.

Padella

You won't mind waiting in line...to get on the waiting list, when the food is this wonderful and prices are this reasonable. The pasta-obsessed flock to this no-reservations, edge-of-Borough-Market pasta bar, where a plate of Pici Cacio e Pepe is a must and Aperitivi are a steal, with affordable spritzes, Negroni and Prosecco by the glass. It's ideal for a cozy carb fix as well as dinner and catching up.

Gloria

The first London restaurant from Big Mamma Group, whose Paris venues have dominated the city's dining scene, is all about the good times. Gloria, a parody of a 1950s trattoria transferred to a Shoreditch street corner, is daring but impossible to resist. Truffled burrata, creamy carbonara artistically blended inside a wheel of pecorino, or a tangle of Mafalda pasta laden with black truffles are just a few of the dishes on the menu.

Ottolenghi

You'll know what you're getting into if you've ever opened one of Yotam Ottolenghi's cookbooks. Food is vibrant and spicy, with a Middle Eastern influence yet an openness to new ideas, while wines are natural-leaning and sourced from small growers. Before you go, pick up some supplies from the deli, including jars of fragrant dukkah and za'atar as well as the lemon and vanilla marmalade.

40 Maltby Street

It's all about the natural wines and the serious talent in the kitchen at 40 Maltby Street, where trains rumble overhead and the decor's strictly DIY (a tiny kitchen, home-made tables, and wine festival posters on the walls). You'll find a scribbled blackboard by the bar, listing the menu—it changes daily. The wines are all sourced from small-scale producers, and there are half-a-dozen options by the glass and eight pages of bottles. Come here for a wine-fueled weekend lunch, with the Maltby market in full swing outside. Just know that they don't take reservations.

Bright London

The owners of Bright made their name with P.Franco, a 12-seat wine bar in Clapton. The pét-nats were first rate and the food was even better, cooked on a two-ring hob by game-for-the-challenge guest chefs. Their follow-up, Bright, is in the hinterlands of London Fields. The airy, pared-back bar and restaurant—this time with a proper kitchen—is where locals drop in with their kids during the day. By night, the room gleams with candlelight and the drinks keep flowing until midnight. The cooking is unshowy but delicious, from charcoal-grilled mackerel to impeccably fresh crudités, served with a luscious, chlorophyll-green parsley and parmesan dip. If ingredients sound challenging, it's worth taking a chance on them, like the tagliatelle, topped with chicken-offal ragu.

Claude Bosi at Bibendum

This is the ideal setting for a lavish supper, beginning with champagne and clever amuse-bouche and ending with a show-stopping cheese trolley. Tables fill up weeks in advance, and the seven-course tasting menu, which combines exquisitely complex dishes with rustic French cooking, creates a palpable sense of anticipation. The meal is remarkable, and the service is flawless and formal. The sommelier is quite helpful. Even the set lunch menu has a magnificent sense about it.

Scully St James's

Pastrami with butterscotch horseradish or cauliflower with salted egg yolk sauce are examples of Scully St James's fusion of flavors and cultures. What's even stranger is it works; we've never had broccoli or a salad with coconut and green strawberries like his. Even seemingly frivolous nibbles, such as dry beef-tendon crackers topped with cloud-like oyster emulsion, require a lot of effort. Because the portions are large, order a main dish to share and then choose from the innovative, nicely displayed desserts.

The Wolseley

With its glittering marble floors, red-and-gold Japanese panels, and sleek leather banquettes, this enormous all-day café oozes a heady grandeur, set in a 1920s car dealership. Londoners come for breakfast and the newspaper, with a menu including anything from stacked pancakes to an Arnold Bennett omelet piled with smoked haddock and creamy hollandaise. Drop over on a whim for just about anything you desire in the majestic settings that never feel too stiffly formal.

Worst Restaurants

The Crypt

Grace Dent, a food critic for the London Evening Standard, was unable to write a comprehensive assessment of Gremio de Brixton because she

did not want to relive the anguish of her visit. "Refused to pay for the food because none was served for hours and what seemed to be still frozen," she wrote. "I started to believe I was being filmed by a BBC3 hidden camera parody."

A. Wong

"Six pretty huge floppy dim sum were assigned to us." Dent murmured sadly, 'They taste like Marks & Spencer's sausage flesh.' Citrus foam was used to coat two of the Xiao long bao. I don't have enough room in this essay to completely express my feelings about foam. But, in a nutshell... can you all stop it?"

The Keeper's House

"If a restaurant is like an orchestra with a lot of people doing very important, different things brilliantly to make something wonderful happen, then The Keeper's House is like listening to Les Dawson clank through Roll Out the Barrel."

Bo London

"Any attempts to converse with your dinner companion will be thwarted by a waiter delivering two additional spoons of Bushtucker-trial gloop, symbolizing the chef's psychological collapse." This is not a meal. Its delectable immersive art caters to a one-of-a-kind clientele of well-heeled tourists and freeloading bloggers."

Galeto

"I'm off to Galeto, a new Brazilian restaurant on Dean Street, to have 'Rio's legendary seductive chicken.' Chicken isn't sexy, according to this bold remark. Not even The Muppets' wicked characters who wore artificial eyelashes.

Chotto Matte

"It must be common for diners to have no idea what Nikkei-Japanese dining is, or what the menu, which is divided into 'chicharronia,' 'cocine client,' 'Nikkei,' 'anticucheria,' and the more obvious 'sushi,' is offering, so it will be reassuring for them to arrive and discover the waiting staff — of which there are approximately 789 — don't.

Paesan

"It's peasant food, like peasants eat, right?" Well, they do if they're those charming bright Continental kitchen-savvy peasants who Jamie Oliver and Rick Stein invariably run into when they arrive in Brindisi."

Bird of Smithfield

"The service was horrible in every sense of the term. It was a master class in what should never happen at a £140 dinner. We asked for every detail of the meal, from placing orders to receiving forks to reading the dessert menu... Our table was scheduled for 9.15pm; pudding arrived about 11.30pm. I tried to pay the bill, but I was no longer visible."

The Pearson Room

"A 'salad' of borlotti and wide beans appeared with the wonderfully nice Romney Marsh lamb chop, which looked like two cans crudely mixed together with a fork. My rule of thumb for restaurant owners is if I can cook more artistically and deftly than you, you're in trouble."

Best Hotels

The Connaught

The Connaught's 19th-century red-brick front is as instantly recognized as the odd water feature outside: Silence, a sculpture by Japanese architect Tadao Ando seeps a mist of water into the air every fifteen minutes. The 3,000-strong collection of unique artworks by artists such as Damien Hirst, Louise Bourgeois and Barbara Hepworth will thrill art lovers even more.

The rooms are modern in design and seem light and airy. Expect marble televisions, a heated toilet seat and cutting-edge audiovisual technology. It's also a foodie's paradise. The hotel boasts an excellent restaurant from Hélène Darroze (two Michelin stars) which underwent a full refurbishment in 2019.

When you see the cobalt-blue, hand-carved front door of The Apartment, you know you're in for a treat: Inside the 3,070-square-foot penthouse, you'll find double-height ceilings with a fireplace, a four-poster king bed in the master bedroom, a guest bedroom, two-and-a-half bathrooms, a large living room, dining room with seating for eight, separate kitchen, large wraparound balcony and two terraces.

The Dorchester

The Dorchester is an iconic part of British heritage and a world-renowned landmark on London's glamorous Park Lane. A 1930s art deco exterior houses 250 rooms and suites designed with classic English interiors, plus three contemporary roof suites with wraparound outdoor terraces overlooking the London skyline. The on-site restaurant Alain Ducasse at The Dorchester is one of only three London restaurants to boast three-Michelin-stars while The Grill at The Dorchester also benefitted from a relaunch in 2019. The Bar at The Dorchester is also led by expert mixologists, who have served many celebrity guests including Tom Cruise, Johnny Depp, the late Michael Jackson, Mariah Carey and Lady Gaga.

The Harlequin Penthouse features silk and leather furnishings, a standalone bath, a fireplace and a spacious outside terrace with panoramic views of London. The design of these suites is subtly reminiscent of the Hollywood glamour that has long been associated with the hotel, while staying fresh, modern and sumptuous. In fact, it was in this room Elizabeth Taylor learned she would feature in the film Cleopatra, and the original pink marble bathroom was built for her use is still in use today.

The Corinthia

The Corinthia debuted in April 2011, offering the largest standard rooms and suites in the bustling metropolis, as well as the luxury brand's uncompromising attention to detail and superb service.

You're in walking distance of the city's biggest landmarks and state buildings, as well as a quick 15-minute taxi journey to the city It is on a lovely quiet street with no shops right off Trafalgar Square and the Thames. The Corinthia London has been masterfully built packed with the best amenities, including one of the best spas in the city, ESPA and famous chef Tom Kerridge's magnificent British cuisine.

The two-story Royal Suite, London's largest, will envelop visitors in luxurious comfort and timeless elegance. Enter through an oval rotunda into a curved living room with panoramic views and a large, 10-seater dining room with a gold-leaf ceiling appropriate for the regalest of occasions. Luxuriate in a stunning master bedroom—located in a turret along with a dressing room—featuring a heavenly bed, views of the Thames and London Eye. It offers a terrace with fire-pit to keep you warm on cooler days.

Brown's Hotel

Brown's Hotel, owned and run by Rocco Forte, is located in the heart of London's Mayfair, just a short distance from Bond Street. Brown's is London's first hotel, having opened its doors in 1837 and counting monarchs, Oscar winners and singers among its previous visitors. It was also where inventor Alexander Graham Bell made the world's first telephone call. The hotel's age adds to its attractiveness, with creaking floors and tiny passageways giving it a sense of history.

Rudyard Kipling is supposed to have written The Jungle Book while staying at Brown's Hotel, which is another amazing anecdote. In honor of the novelist, the hotel has named its most prestigious suite after him. Residents are greeted with a statue of a cheeky monkey outside the entrance door as part of the homage. Several framed handwritten letters from the author are included in the suite, as well as other references to Kipling.

The Langham

The Langham has a storied hotel history which dates back to 1865, when it opened as Europe's first Grand Hotel. This flagship hotel has been at the forefront of refined and polite hospitality for nearly 140 years. It has occupied an unmatched location in the heart of London since its inception. This is still the case today. It is one of London's most centrally positioned luxury hotels, with a location at the top of Regent Street and a short walk to Bond Street.

The Infinity spacious two-bedroom suite overlooks All Souls Church and features a master bedroom with inviting four-poster bed and two dressing rooms, a second bedroom with ensuite, separate lobby and cloakroom, kitchen, bespoke furniture and the latest Bose audio technology to enhance each guest's experience. The suite also features a stunning infinity bath providing the ultimate spa-like comfort. To deliver the ultimate chromotherapy experience, the infinity bath cleanses, revitalizes and harnesses the strong impact of colors on mood.

7 Affordable Hotels in London

Best for West End excitement: Assembly Hotel London

This is one of the most centrally located in London, right between the National Gallery and the always-bustling Leicester Square. Fashion designers such as Gareth Pugh and Alexander McQueen have influenced the aesthetic. The rooftop Garden Room, which serves breakfast, cocktails and everything in between, is located on the tenth story.

Best for Michelin-starred cuisine: Town Hall Hotel, Bethnal Green

The destination restaurant, two Michelin-starred Da Terra, has been a hit on the east London food scene since it first opened in what was previously a town hall in 2010. Brazilian chef Rafael Cagali serves South American-inspired tasting menus here, while the Corner Room provides breakfast and more casual bistro-style dishes. Start the day with a swim in the light-filled pool, which has original period elements or loft-style aesthetics.

Best for viewing from a rooftop garden: The Buxton

This charming bar and hotel, named for local anti-slavery activist and social reformer Sir Thomas Fowell Buxton, is located on Brick Lane. Handwoven artworks, carpets and blankets and a selection of books picked by adjacent bookseller Libreria adorn the 15 sparse but practical rooms. The ground-floor bar and restaurant specialize in British and European meals like pan-fried gnocchi with Jerusalem artichoke or duck breast with beetroot puree. There's a guests-only rooftop garden with stunning views of the city.

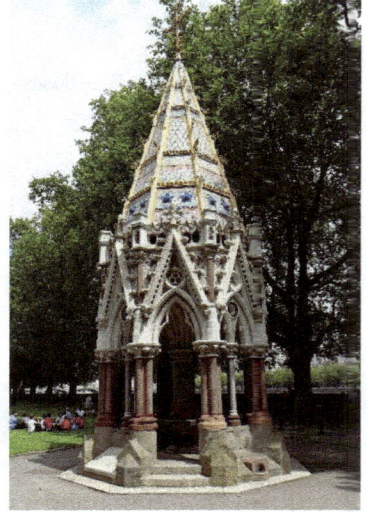

Family-friendly: Moxy London Stratford

From the bicycle on the wall to the silhouettes of athletes swimming skipping and playing table tennis etched onto wood paneling in the lobby living area, Moxy London Stratford has a vague sports motif. A reference to its position ten minutes' walk from the Queen Elizabeth Olympic Park. Families are encouraged to remain there by table football, novels and board londongames (as well as the bar), while the 24-hour grab-and-go is ideal for stocking up on supplies before venturing out.

Best for visiting museums: The Rockwell, Kensington

It's convenient location, right by the blockbuster museums and boutique shopping in Chelsea, that makes it a winner. Inside the Victorian townhouse, the look is classic. The rooms are furnished with floral wallpapers and oak furniture. Another boon is the walled garden, dotted with pretty plants and ideal for alfresco summer drinks. The restaurant serves an all-day brunch menu.

Best for sightseeing and shopping: The Z Hotel, Covent Garden

The no-frills, function-first Z Hotel group has 11 locations throughout the capital, but this one, a red-brick house behind the Piazza in Covent Garden, stands out for its lively, wonderful location. The rooms are small, but they offer pristine sheets and comfortable beds. In the evenings, there's a café serving continental breakfast and complimentary cheese and wine, making it a great aperitivo stop.

Best for location: The Pilgrm, Paddington

Across the street from Paddington station, The Pilgrm is spread across four Victorian houses which have been beautifully and sensitively restored: think reclaimed cast iron radiators, mid-century armchairs and wooden parquet flooring. The smallest rooms are the bunks (no televisions); all come with charming white-tiled utilitarian bathrooms, Marshall Bluetooth speakers, a selection of books and artwork on the walls; ask for a room at the back of the hotel to avoid the noise of London Street. Communal pantries replace room service and there's The Lounge for brunch, coffee and killer cocktails. Grab a table on the balcony-style terrace for people watching.

The Best Hotels in London for Each Category

Best For Affordable Hospitality: Point A Liverpool Street

Point A is a tiny, family-run business with six London locations that aims to "bring hospitality back into the cheap space." Sushi Samba and Duck and Waffle are also a 10-minute walk from the Liverpool Street location, as is the Queen of Hoxton nightlife destination. The Hypnos bed, power shower, 40-inch Smart TV, hairdryer and mood lighting are all included in the compact, minimalist rooms. Guests can use a nearby high-end gym for free throughout their stay by showing their room key card.

Best for Food and Drink: Hoxton Southwark

This bustling addition to the hinterland between Southwark and Blackfriars is located on formerly dingy Blackfriars Road. It has the same Hoxton recipe as the others, with a large lobby full with movers and shakers doing everything from working with little coffees to ordering after-work cocktails. There is plenty of mid-century velvet furniture and view-obstructing plants. It's hard to think individuals come here to sleep on a Friday evening. A DJ blasts club music into the cocktail bar and downstairs restaurant, Albie, which serves French-Italian fusion meals. The staff greets you at check-in wearing grey marl branded Hoxton sweatshirts.

Best for Sleek Style in the Heart of the Action: Z Hotel Tottenham Court Road

This branch of the Z Hotel group is smack bang in the midst of the action if you're searching for the West End and the stores of Oxford Street, with a pricing that's more suburban than city center. Despite its prime location, the 120-room old office building hasn't forgotten about aesthetics, with stylish, contemporary rooms in white and charcoal. Despite their coziness, all rooms have an ensuite shower room, pristine bed linen and a Samsung 49-inch HD Smart TV. There are no windows in the cheapest rooms.

Best For Mixing Business with Pleasure: Citizen M London Bankside

This Amsterdam-based brand is aimed squarely at the younger demographic, guaranteeing "absolutely no trouser presses, bellboys, or silly pillow chocolates." Instead, it has an XL king-sized bed, a wall-to-wall window, a rain shower, and complimentary movies in each room.

There are also free to use iMacs dotted around the lobby, making it an ideal spot for remote working. Guests will find a powerful hairdryer in their room, plus specially tailored am and pm toiletries to suit their body clock. Bedrooms are all minimal chic while the lobby is decked out with trendy Vitra furniture. Citizen M is conveniently positioned near Borough Market, the Globe, and the Shard, as well as everything else London Bridge has to offer. Breakfast is extra at the 24-hour Canteen M.

Best For Design-Hotel Chic Away from the Crowds: Hotel 55

Hotel 55 is well-connected while remaining away from the noise, being only one minute from North Ealing tube station. The rooms at this non-chain boutique hotel contain original artwork, trendy mismatched furniture and vividly painted walls in green and blue. A king size bed, huge screen TV, hairdryer, L'Occitane amenities, and complementary magazines are included in the "cozy" room. Momo, the hotel's modern Japanese restaurant, has views of the hotel's beautiful garden.

Best for home-from-home decadence: Rockwell East

This aparthotel blurs the boundary between self-catering apartments and a full hotel, with 57 studios, one-bed and family-sized units available. With vivid splashes of royal blue and saffron, the décor is stylish and playful. Each self-contained apartment includes a fully equipped kitchen, dishwasher, washer/dryer, and HDTV. Rockwell East is distinguished by its extra touches, which include Merino wool blankets, Egyptian cotton linens, toweling dressing gowns, White Company amenities, a Nespresso coffee machine along with an Abel and Cole welcome breakfast pack. It's a short walk from Tower Bridge and has an all-day café and bar operating from seven in the morning to midnight.

Best for Booze Before Bed: The Culpeper

The Culpeper is a bar with rooms rather than a full hotel, but it's not your typical sticky-floored old man's boozer. Natural wines, local ales and cocktails created with herbs grown on the roof garden are on the beverages list. The quaint hotel bares brick and flattering lighting. Deep fried black pudding balls, eggplant parmigiana and beer-battered haddock are among the items served by the first-floor kitchen. This reassuringly traditional pub fare with a gastro twist. A selection of five tastefully decorated bedrooms awaits you on the second floor, merging the modern – buffed concrete walls – with the more traditional, such as custom oak headboards. The nearby Aldgate East station is an excellent starting point for exploring Whitechapel and Shoreditch.

Best For Bohemian Chic: My Bloomsbury

My Hotels is an economical boutique hotel brand with two locations – one in London and the other in Brighton – that excels in terms of design. The Bloomsbury location is ideal, situated between Goodge Street and Tottenham Court Road stations. It features 86 rooms, a coworking space, award-winning artisan baker Gail's, and a Body Kalm treatment area for those looking to relax after a day of touring. A variety of luxurious furnishings from labels such as Conran Design and Heal's liven up the bedrooms. Each room has a multi-channel flat screen LCD TV and a workstation. The bathrooms are furnished with eco-friendly Pure Lakes shower supplies.

Best Time to Visit London

March through May is the greatest time to visit London since the weather is moderate and the city's parks are green and blossoming. Late spring and summer, on the other hand, are peak tourist seasons. Hotel and airfare prices reflect this.

London's temperate climate allows visitors to come at any time of year.

The weather in spring can be moderate but damp, and the Easter weekend offers various closures as well as celebrations to be mindful of. Summer comes with it music festivals, outdoor movies, and a plethora of other exciting outdoor activities. Autumn is frequently pleasant. Despite the weather, the Christmas season in London is certainly worth seeing, followed by fantastic New Year's Eve celebrations and, of course, the January bargains.

London is accessible at any time of year due to its temperate environment and lack of harsh weather. However, depending on the season, your visit will be different.

Spring: March to May

Springtime in London brings extended daylight hours and warm weather, with temperatures ranging from 52° to 59°F. Traveling with an umbrella is still recommended, as spring showers are prevalent.

Good Friday and Easter Monday are also public holidays during this time. Most stores are closed on Easter Sunday, and public transportation services may be impacted.

Over the Easter weekend and for the two-week Easter holiday, Central London is packed.

Summer: June to August

Summer is a terrific season to visit because the weather is nice and you can enjoy London's green spaces, beer gardens and rooftop bars. The average temperature is 64°F, with highs of 86°F — ideal for attending one of London's summer music festivals or outdoor theaters.

Summer is the most popular time of year to visit London due to the pleasant weather and school holidays. To avoid lines, book attractions ahead of time.

Autumn: September to November

In the second week of September, the summer season draws to a close. Autumn is a great season to visit London since the weather is moderate, ranging from 52° to 59°F. There are many annual events to enjoy such as the Totally Thames festival and Halloween celebrations. From November onwards, you can admire the stunning Christmas lights and decorations.

Taking advantage of the school vacations, the October half-term is one of the most popular times for families to visit.

Winter: December to February

Despite the fact London is colder in the winter, typical temperatures of 36° to 43°F ensure you'll be able to fully enjoy the city – just bundle up warm!

The Christmas lights, decorations and activities taking place throughout December are an added bonus. From Christmas Eve through New Year's Day, make sure to check public transportation in advance because there may be engineering work and decreased service. Remember to shop the January sales, which begin just after Christmas.

January and February are normally calmer times of year to visit. You can often find lower prices on accommodation, activities and restaurants.

March – May

London's peak tourist season lasts all year, but late spring (and summer) are extremely busy. By visiting London in late spring, you'll be able to see the royal parks and gardens in bloom, as well as take advantage of the city's ideal weather. However, the earlier you go in spring, the less likely you are to encounter crowds. While fall and winter can be especially rainy, summer can get a bit muggy, spring in London enjoys a happy medium, with average temps hovering between the 50s and 60s.

Key Events:

- Vault Festival (late January-March)
- St Patrick's Day Festival and Parade (March)
- London Coffee Festival (March-April)
- Gemini Boat Race (April)
- London Book Fair (April)
- State Opening of Parliament (May)
- Hackney Moves (May)
- RHS Chelsea Flower Show (May)

June - August

The tourist crowds are made a little more acceptable by the pleasant summer temps (mid-70s). Summer also brings little break from rain and the resulting humidity. An umbrella is a must-have item.

Key Events:

- Trooping the Colour (June)
- London Pride (June-July)
- Wimbledon Championships (June-July)
- Kaleidoscope (July)
- Underbelly Festival (July-September)
- Notting Hill Carnival (August)

September – November

Thanks to the moderate 60–70-degree temperatures. London is still packed with tourists well into September. Not to mention the gorgeous autumn foliage. This is, however, the greatest time to visit if you want to completely immerse yourself in the culture. The annual events in these months, particularly Guy Fawkes Night in November, are deeply established in not only London but also England's history.

Key Events:

- London Fashion Week
- London Marathon
- Guy Fawkes Night
- The Lord Mayor's Show
- Christmas at Kew

December - February

If you want to save a few pounds, travel during the cold winter months (except for December when rates rise around the holidays). Though temps are expected to be in the 30s and 40s, you'll be able to enjoy a more real London experience without the crowds. Because the city twinkles with glittering lights and festivities during the Christmas season, central London is typically packed with holiday shoppers, particularly on Oxford Street. If you're visiting London for the holidays, plan to see the city's Christmas decorations away from the tourist traps.

Key Events:

- Christmas at Kew (November-January)
- London's New Year's Day Parade (First of January)
- Burns Night (January)
- Pancake Day (February/March)

4 Days in Los Angeles Travel Itinerary

Day 1

Toast Bakery Cafe, Beverly Hills, The Walk of fame and the famous theaters, Hollywood Sign and Griffifth Observatory

Day 2

Santa Monica, Venice, Roadtrip to Malibu for sunset

Day 3

Brunch on Sunset, Museums in Los Angeles, La Brea Tarpits Museum, Petersen Automotive Museum

Day 4

Universal Studios Hollywood

4-Day Travel Itinerary

Know Before You Go

Money

A 4-day budget in London (excluding transportation and lodging): $315 per day.

The British Pound Sterling (GBP, £), also known as "pounds" or "quid," is the currency of England. Aside from a few street food carts, there aren't really any cash-only establishments in London.

However, having pounds on hand for tipping is always a good idea, as service is not often included in bills. Because paper bills don't start at £5, it's essential to bring a coin purse with you.

London, like Paris and New York, is a notoriously pricey city. Though there are methods to save money in London, hotels, restaurants and drink will come at a premium.

The advantage of shopping in London is VAT is already incorporated. The price on the tag/menu is the price you'll pay.

Transport

Despite the concerns of Londoners, the Underground (also known as "the tube") is normally a relatively efficient mode of transportation. During your four days in London, you'll use public transportation extensively, including buses, overground trains and the tube.

As a result, getting an Oyster card as soon as you arrive in London is critical.

These contactless cards make it simple to use public transportation. To pay for your journey, simply load money into the card and touch it on the round yellow readers. For trains and the tube, you tap in and out at gates, but for buses, you only tap in.

You may purchase an Oyster card at any London airport, train station or tube station. They are located outside the escalators/elevators that lead to the subway in airports. Some machines only accept cash, although the majority accept debit and credit cards.

Before embarking on your 4-day London schedule, you should definitely download the Citymapper app. It's fantastic for determining the optimal public transportation routes from point A to point B. It's also updated in real time, so delays or closures won't catch you off guard.

Day 1: Belgravia, Mayfair, Westminster, & Embankment

You won't want to rush into busy tourist attractions after a lengthy and presumably packed journey into the city. Instead, you'll begin your four-day London trip in the lovely Belgravia neighborhood.

Belgravia is one of London's most beautiful areas, located just west of Victoria Station. It's also one of the greatest places to find the best London presents.

There are no significant tourist attractions here, however there are a few places on your Belgravia walking tour you won't want to miss:

- **Peggy Porschen's pink and floral exterior** is undoubtedly London's most photographed location. Expect a huge line if you want to try their famed sweets.
- **Moyses Stevens Flowers** is tastefully adorned. They change their

entrance display every couple months with vibrant flowers.

- Halkin Mews is wonderful all year, but the spring and summer blooms really bring it to life. When you visit, please be calm and considerate of the residents.
- Orange Square is the neighborhood's beating heart, with weekly markets and locally owned businesses.
- Wilton Crescent is a curving stretch of elegant residences that looks a lot like Bath's Royal Crescent.

Hyde Park

Hyde Park is a large green park in London's centre. Families are picnicking, horses are running down the pathways, and pedal boats are gliding along the Serpentine.

Don't try to see the entire park, because you won't have enough time. Instead, stick to the eastern half, which includes the unique Princess Diana Memorial Fountain.

If you're visiting London in winter, Hyde Park will be a very different place. December sees the place transformed into Winter Wonderland, complete with an ice rink and carnival rides.

After your stroll, head east through the Wellington Arch towards Buckingham Palace.

Buckingham Palace

It's time to visit the city's most tourist-heavy spot after a laid-back sample of London life.

Buckingham Palace is closed to the public for the majority of the year. As a result, this trip on the London itinerary is primarily for viewing the outside and taking photos.

Buckingham Palace, on the other hand, is open from late July until September. Tickets must be booked in advance for a designated time slot. The standard tour costs £25 and the more extended "Royal Day Out" costs £45.

You can purchase tickets and have them delivered to you online. You can also print and exchange your ticket vouchers on location. Using the voucher approach, however, requires standing in a (often) long line, which takes time away from your four days in London.

Trafalgar Square

Trafalgar Square is alive with activity at all times of the day. People can be seen relaxing on the National Gallery's steps, meeting friends by the fountains, and passing by on their way to Charing Cross station.

If you have some additional time, visit the National Gallery for free to see some world-famous artworks. Otherwise, take in the sights and sounds of the city before traveling south to Westminster Abbey.

Westminster Abbey

Westminster Abbey is a must-see for anybody interested in architecture, history, or literature. For nearly 1,000 years, this Gothic masterpiece has hosted England's coronations and royal weddings.

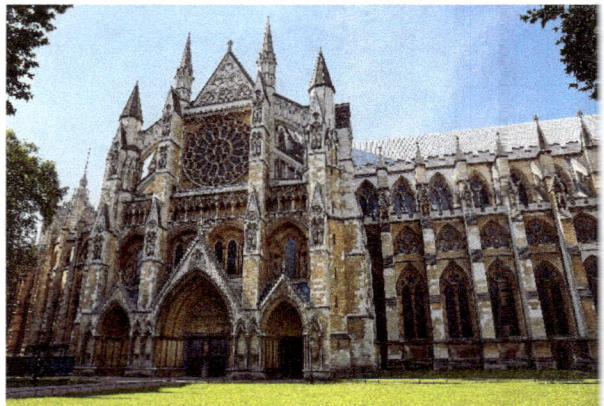

It also holds the graves of some of the country's most famous figures, including Elizabeth I, Sir Isaac Newton, and Charles Dickens.

Because of the enormous lines, I strongly advise purchasing tickets in advance online.

If you start your London itinerary on a Wednesday, however, you may get a "Wednesday Lates" entrance for £11 in person from 4:30-6pm.

Embankment

Finish your first of four days in London with a stroll along the Thames in the evening. The London Eye and other features of the London skyline may be seen clearly from Embankment.

There are various tube and railway stations along the road, so you can walk as far as you want. You might also go to the outdoor Southbank Centre Book Market to pick up some books set in London, depending on the time.

When you're ready to eat, there are plenty of excellent pubs and restaurants near Embankment and Blackfriars stations. For Mexican, I recommend Lupita Central, and for Japanese, I recommend Hare & Tortoise.ankment

Day 2: City of London & Southwark

Leadenhall Market

Fans of Harry Potter will identify Leadenhall Market as a Diagon Alley filming location.

It's like stepping back in time when you walk through this covered Victorian market. Taking a glance around will convince you that this is one of the best non-touristy things to do in London. The businesses of Leadenhall Market are a mix of modern and historic, despite the antique building. Most places don't open until after 10 a.m., but photographing the neighborhood in the morning is much easier.

Exit the market and head east on Fenchurch Ave, looking for the sleek new entrance to The Garden at 120 on your right.

The Garden at 120

First opened in February 2019, the Garden at 120 is London's newest public rooftop with a view. Unlike the Sky Garden, you don't need a reservation for these amazing and free panoramic views of London.

Visiting hours begin at 10 a.m., and you must first clear security before boarding the elevator. There are currently only benches and plants on the roof, but there are plans to open a bar and restaurant in the future.

However, because of the unique vistas of the city's prominent monuments, it's still a must-see on your 4-day London itinerary.

Return to the Tower of London by descending the elevator and walking south.

Tower of London and Tower Bridge

To be honest, the Tower of London isn't far from being a tourist trap. Even the yeoman warders don't hide their feelings. Despite the price, the crowds, and the guided tours (which I typically despise), the Tower of London is a terrific place to visit.

While you can explore the area on your own, I recommend the free Yeoman Warder excursions. These individuals are more than just tour guides; they served in the British military before being appointed to the Tower. If you get Billy, you'll receive a dose of history mixed up with plenty of snarky English humor.

You can skip the big line and get straight to the ticket exchange counter if you buy tickets in advance online. The line to purchase tickets at the gate can be very long! After seeing the Tower,

proceed south to the Tower Bridge, which spans the Thames. A waterside pedestrian route continues west towards the Globe Theatre once you've crossed.

Shakespeare's Globe

It would be crazy to visit London without at least walking past Shakespeare's Globe Theatre. Though the original burned down a long time ago, this authentic replica is a must see.

If you do opt for a tour, it's best to book ahead online. It takes about 30 minutes for the guided tour and another 45 minutes to see the exhibition.

Borough Market

Foodies will rejoice at Borough Market, where local vendors sell everything from artisanal truffles to exotic spices. There are restaurants all along the outside, with food stalls mixed throughout the space. I highly recommend the paella and the pie stand.

Many places are cash only, so bring plenty of quid if you want to eat and shop. The market is open every day except Sundays, though some stalls are closed Mondays and Tuesdays.

St. Paul's Cathedral

In all of London, St. Paul's is my favorite location. It amazingly survived WWII bombardment and now serves as a beacon of hope and perseverance.

With ceiling frescoes, golden accents, and ornate doors, the building is stunning both inside and out. Lord Nelson, Duke of Wellington, and Sir Christopher Wren, the famed London architect, are both buried there.

The fact that you may climb the dome for spectacular views of London is something that many tourists are unaware of. The climb to the top includes about 500 stairs, however there are a few rest stops along the route, including a Whispering Gallery.

St. Paul's last admission hour is 4 p.m., so plan your visit accordingly. You may save £3 on advance tickets by purchasing them online instead than paying £20 at the door. Faster entrance is available with online tickets, and you can enter at any moment during the day.

Day 3: Notting Hill, Kensington, & Regent's Park

Notting Hill

Exploring Notting Hill is one of the most popular things to do in London for first-timers, thanks to the eponymous film and Instagram.

The vividly colored row residences and popular Portobello Road market attract the majority of visitors. But if you know where to look, there's more to see.

Here are some highlights and hidden gems to visit on your Notting Hill walking tour, starting at Ladbroke Grove tube station:

- St. Luke's Mews might be the prettiest residences in all of London, with pastel painted homes and cobblestone pavers.
- Lancaster Road is home to the iconic row of bold, colorful houses you often see in photos of Notting Hill.
- Ladbroke Walk is one vibrant strip of cute homes that hasn't been overrun by Instagrammers (yet).

- Portobello Road Market is the world's largest antique market, with stalls and brick-and-mortar shops lining both sides of the road. On Fridays and Saturdays, international food stalls sell everything from Peruvian sandwiches to Jamaican jerk chicken.
- The Prince Edward pub caters to locals and tourists alike, with tasty food and fun bookshelf print wallpaper.
- The Churchill Arms knows how to show off: this pub's facade is always decked out in florals, and boasts dozens of tiny Christmas trees in December.

Photography in Notting Hill: When taking photos of Notting Hill's colorful streets, please be respectful. At no point should you trespass on someone's property (i.e. go on their porch, sit on the steps, etc.).

You're only a few blocks west of Kensington Palace when you finish at The Churchill Arms.

Kensington Palace

Kensington Palace is surprisingly available to tourists for the most of the year. However, you'll stay on the outside for this four-day London itinerary.

As you go east through Kensington Gardens, towards Exhibition Road, take in the front and side views of Queen

Victoria's birthplace. Then head south to the free museum district.

Regent's Park

You'll be ready to unwind at Regent's Park after a hard day. This regal location is attractive all year, out the rose garden of Queen Mary shines brightest in the summer.

You can go up to Primrose Hill for spectacular views of the London skyline if you're not completely exhausted.

Day 4: Hampstead, & Covent Garden

Hampstead Village

You should have a flavor of local life before your four days in London are through. You'll forget you're in the city when you visit Hampstead.

There is no specific sightseeing to be done here, like there is in Belgravia. Take a leisurely stroll through the alleyways and up the main street instead.

For your Hampstead walking tour, here are a few must-see locations:

- Coffee is served from a refurbished red telephone booth at Kape Barako.
- Perrin's Lane and Flask Walk are photogenic streets with attractive stores and cafes.
- Burgh House, which also serves as the Hampstead Museum, offers garden views and Edwardian beauty.
- When you've had your fill of rural charm, head north to Hampstead Heath through the stately Downshire Hill.

Hampsted Heath

One of London's largest green parks is Hampstead Heath. Residents enjoy the public swimming ponds all year, and walking trails weave through woodlands and farms. The Parliament Hill overlook offers panoramic views of London.

Check Google Maps or Citymapper for the best path to the British Library after your walk. A bus may be the best option depending on where you exit Hampstead Heath.

Covent Garden

Covent Garden is a bustling shopping and dining district in central London. You could easily spend an entire day here and still not see everything.

There's much to see and do even if you're not a big spender. Here are some of the highlights in the area:

- Check out Seven Dials' seven radial streets, which are especially festive around Christmas.
- Neal's Yard is a vibrant courtyard filled with chic boutiques and eateries.
- The covered market in Covent Garden is lovely all year, but in December it is the most gorgeous site in London (see above photo)
- The Royal Opera House's menagerie-like glass entryway will appeal to architecture fans.
- Rules is one of London's swankiest and oldest restaurants, with candlelight tables and high-end British cuisine.
- Get a drink at the Lamb & Flag, an 18th-century pub that Charles Dickens visited.

Budgeting for London

What amount of cash will you require for your vacation to London?

You should budget $182 a day for your trip in London, as this is the average daily price based on other guests' costs. Previous tourists spent an average of £29 ($36) on meals and £21 ($26) on local transportation in one day. In addition, the average hotel cost for a couple in London is £181 ($228). As a result, a one-week trip to London for two people costs on average £2,029 ($2,551). These average travel rates were gathered from other travelers to assist you in planning your own trip budget.

Accomodation Budget in London (Average Daily Costs)

The average cost of accommodation in London for one person is £91. The average hotel room in London costs £181 for two persons sharing a regular double-occupancy room.

Transportation Budget in London(Average Daily Costs)

Taxis in London are much more expensive than public transit. Previous visitors to London have paid an average of £21 per person per day on local transportation.

Food Budget in London (Average Daily Costs)

While meal costs in London vary, the average daily cost of meals is £29 in London. Based on past travelers' spending habits, a typical supper in London should cost roughly £11 per person while dining out. Breakfast is frequently less expensive than lunch or dinner. Food in sit-down restaurants in London is frequently more expensive than quick cuisine or street food.

Entertainment Budget in London (Average Daily Costs)

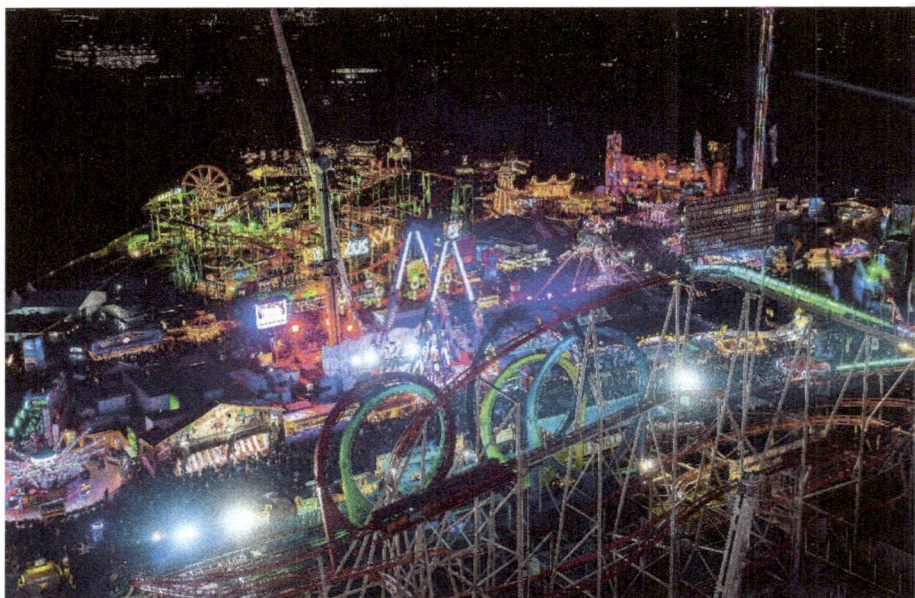

The average cost of entertainment and activities in London is £26 per person, per day. This covers prices for museum and attraction admission tickets, day tours, and other sightseeing charges.

Tips and Handouts Budget in London (Average Daily Costs)

In London, the average daily cost of Tips and Handouts is £2.68. In London, a tip is usually between 10% and 20%.

Scams, Robberies, and Mishaps Budget in London (Average Daily Costs)

On a journey, however, awful things can happen. Well, you've just got to deal with it! In London, the average cost of a fraud, robbery, or mishap is £15.

Alcohol Budget in London (Average Daily Costs)

In London, the average person spends roughly £12 per day on alcoholic beverages. Despite your bigger budget, the more you spend on booze, the more fun you may have.

Water Budget in London (Average Daily Costs)

In London, people spend £3.23 per day on bottled water on average. London's public water is rated safe to drink.

Photo Credit

Spiroview Inc. – stock.adobe.com – Mayfair district of London, Elegant shops and restaurants, 2016, pg. 2.

SventlanaSF – stock.adobe.com – London, United Kingdom – January 14, 2018: Traditional London black hackney cab or carriage in an empty street in central London, pg. 3.

William – stock.adobe.com – London – March, 2018: Exterior of the Lyceum Theatre, home of the hugely popular and successful Lion King musical in London's West End district, pg. 7.

William – stock.adobe.com – London – City of London and Bank of England / Royal Exchange in the City of London, pg. 8.

Pcruciatti – stock.adobe.com – Entrance door of 10 Downing Street in London on June 16, 2013. The street was built in the 1680s by Sir George Downing and is now the residence of the Prime Minister, pg. 11.

Chrisdorney – stock.adobe.com – The Sherlock Holmes Public House in London, pg. 14.

Alena – stock.adobe.com – London, UK – August 20, 2020: Exterior of a closed Haringey Arms pub in Crouch End, London, UK, pg. 22.

Rixin – stock.adobe.com – London, UK – 7th June 2017: Suits of armour and a display of breastplates in the Armoury of the Tower of London, pg. 23.

Leonid Andronov – stock.adobe.com – The Victoria Memorial and Buckingham Palace in London, England, pg. 26.

Donatas Dabravolskas – stock.adobe.com – London, UK – October 19, 2019: Entrance to the Chinatown area, which is a popular tourist destination in London, pg. 33.

Pxl.store – stock.adobe.com – Soho, London. A dusk view of the central London former red-light district now better known for its bars, restaurants and night life, pg. 33.

Tony Baggett – stock.adobe.com – London, United Kingdom, April 30, 2011: The Strand London Underground tube station which is no longer in use and is a popular travel destination tourist attraction landmark stock photo image, pg. 40.

Coward_lion – stock.adobe.com – London, UK – May 21, 2018: The sweeping Tulip Stairs are one of the original features of the Queen's House. They were the first geometric self-supporting spiral staircase in Britain, pg. 41.

Richie Chan – stock.adobe.com – night view of King Cross station in London, UK, pg. 42.

EleSi – stock.adobe.com – London, United Kingdom – September 17, 2013: The British Museum in London dedicated to human history and culture was established in 1753, pg. 43.

I-Wei Huang – stock.adobe.com – Neal's Yard, a small colourful alley in London's Covent Garden area, pg. 43.

Pxl.store – stock.adobe.com – The Charles Dickens Museum housed in the authors former home on Doughty Street, Holborn, London, pg. 45.

Jjfarq – stock.adobe.com – Bethnal Green Road and Brick Lane Shorditch, London, pg. 48.

Chris Lawrence – stock.adobe.com – London, UK – September 29, 2018: Vintage market stalls outside Lassco Restaurant in Maltby Street on Market Day, pg. 49.

Kristina Blokhin – stock.adobe.com - London, UK – June 22, 2018: The Royal Academy of Arts Institution at Burlington House on Piccadilly Circus with Arcade, summer exhibitions banners advertising colorful on sunny summer day, pg. 53.

Chris Lawrence – stock.adobe.com – London, UK – August 25, 2018: Façade and sign on The Connaught Hotel in Carlos Place, Mayfair, pg. 55.

Pawel Pajor – stock.adobe.com – London – November, 2018: The Dorchester 5 Star Hotel on London's Park Lane, overlooking Hyde Park. A luxury hotel with bars and a restaurant, pg. 56.

Michael Derrer Fuchs – stock.adobe.com – Luxury Corinthia Hotel at City of Westminster on a cloudy summer day. Photo taken August 3, 2022, London, United Kingdom, pg. 57.

William – stock.adobe.com – London – Bond Street, a landmark street of high end fashion shops in London's West End, pg. 58.

Alena – stock.adobe.com – London, UK – April 13, 2019: Close up of Swiss Glockenspiel musical clock in Swish Court, Leicester Square, London, UK, pg. 60.

Florin – stock.adobe.com – Futuristic signs outside Westfield mall in Stratford, London, pg. 61.

Beataaldridge – stock.adobe.com – London – November 13, 2021: Oxford Street in London is decorated with sparkling stars draped over the length of the street for Christmas this year, pg. 69.

Chrisdorney – stock.adobe.com – Harrods in London, UK, pg. 70.

Chrisdorney – stock.adobe.com – Georgian Architecture on Wilton Crescent in London, UK, pg. 78.

Longfin Media – stock.adobe.com – Borough Market. Famous historic food market hall in Southwark. The Shard skyscraper in background on May 29, 2019 in London, England, United Kingdom, pg. 86.

Mistervlad – stock.adobe.com – Kensington palace and gardens, London, United Kingdom, pg 89.

References

https://www.pexels.com/photo/city-view-at-london-672532/

https://blog.aifsabroad.com/2017/04/07/intro-london-england/

https://www.city-data.com/world-cities/London-Introduction.html

https://www.britannica.com/place/London

https://theworldpursuit.com/facts-about-london/

https://englishstudio.com/essential-english-phrases-london/

https://greatbritishmag.co.uk/uk-culture/top-ten-british-etiquette-tips/

https://www.solosophie.com/secret-spots-in-london-youll-love/

https://www.kinggoya.com/london-food-critic-here-are-the-worst-restaurants/

https://elitetraveler.com/features/best-hotels-in-london

https://www.thetimes.co.uk/travel/destinations/uk/england/london/best-budget-hotels-in-london

https://www.independent.co.uk/travel/hotels/london-best-budget-hotels-cheap-deal-low-price-where-to-stay-uk-b1967634.html

https://www.visitlondon.com/things-to-do/visiting-london-for-the-first-time/best-time-to-visit

https://travel.usnews.com/London_England/When_To_Visit/

https://www.visitlondon.com/things-to-do/family-activities/101-things-to-do-with-kids-in-london

https://theportablewife.com/travel/destinations/london-itinerary-4-days/#londonitinerary

https://www.budgetyourtrip.com/united-kingdom/london